How Many Versions Of Us Exist

ss

Brandi Hankins

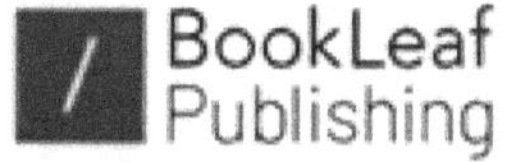

Presentation by *BookLeaf Publishing*

Web: www.bookleafpub.com

E-mail: info@bookleafpub.com

ISBN: 9789357210355

First edition 2022

DEDICATION

To my Husband; for inspiring me, and never getting in the way of my creativity.

PREFACE

Life is hard, and then you die. But hopefully, along the way, you find a reason to stay. I've spent my life finding reasons, and none have been quite so encompassing as love. Love notes and texts from a writer can be quite extra, and my husband suggested I write a book of love notes. So, I did.

What Do We Have Here

When dawn creeps closer, as light peeks through
My heart unfolds and draws nearer to you
Moments pass in sunlit hours
Thoughts turn circles
Missing your presence
Awaiting your return
Such elegance does it no justice
It explains so little despite arduous intent
Our love isn't like that
True love spoken in excitedly hushed tones
Glorified in hardbacked tomes
Maybe it exists
But I need no Prince Charming
With you, my King, I need nothing
In empty room or barren field
It is only you, I require

Are There Any Shadows Left

You ask, and how it pleases me
To give
If I can offer you
Some solace
A rest from world wearies or a moment of peace
I shall try
Mayhap what I offer
Is lesser than others
But my will
My passion
My wellspring of Love
'Tis endless concerning you
If ever a soul
Loved a soul
Its bond would be but a shadow
Cast by our light

Why The Sea Calls

3

You are my rock
May I always be between you, and our hard
places
Let me act as water, smoothing and protecting
You from all hurts

Have no worry to erosion, for the grand master
plan
Requires we both move from seashore to land
Fear not any boulders for they surely will not
stay
Water whittles all of it down day, after day

Together we will be free, to wish and to wander
Crossing vast landscapes with no time to
squander
Until one day they'll find us, apart from it all
The sand and the sea, with our love as the call

Tell Me It All

4

Do any two people gossip as much as we?
Catching up on one another's day
Filling in news and spilling emotions held back
Sharing moments of stress and excitement and
joy
I despise being away, all the day long
But how I adore our times of reconnection
When details big and small, all seem worthwhile
mention

You Don't Diminish, You Enhance

I love our children
I love our life
But best of all
I love being your wife

Falling Feels Like Flying
With You

You're a better person than I
You know how I know?
You rarely judge or criticize me
I do so all the time
I may regret it instantly
But you should surely know
I love you most despite it all

Know that I see your sacrifices
With both our backs against the wall
We face every challenge as a team
So, I'm never worried if we fall

Lullaby

Tell me of the ways you love me
Remind me of who I am
Comfort lives inside those arms
Safe haven, don't you see
Cuddle round and hold on tight
Moments are not lost on me
Breathing sounds to lull my sleep
Hold me while I count on sheep

You Be You, Thanks For Letting Me Be Me

You will know you've found one
When you can be more yourself
When their presence is always missed
When you finally let yourself, be

My Kind Of Weird

Sweaty and silly in road bike getup
You were amusing, for sure
Disc golfing with our boys
You were kind, funny, still pretty weird
But then, so am I
The call from your ex
She just wanted you out from underfoot
But friends help friends and
She said you hadn't any
I could help with that
I offered to hang, let you suggest
You said I know it's odd but
I'd really love to just play with your hair
So, Bob's Burgers and straight soft hair
My head in your lap
My hand on your leg
My face looking up at yours
Grandma's pumpkin pie nearby
You tried again
Ever since then
We've been happily more than friends

Love You Mostest

I love you like there's no tomorrow and
All we have is today
It's a fierce, burning obsession
That never really goes away
You, lying bare and comfortable
Contentment bleeding through your pores
You are my happy space and
All the spaces in between
Not a day goes by that I don't wish
I could spend every second with you
Even knowing absence grows fondness
Your soul plus mine, equals bliss
Maybe Hollywood sets high standards for love
But you exceed every single one

Embodiment

In quiet moments
I know I am loved
By God, sure
But by you, Indefinitely
Maybe God's love is unrelenting
But he requires things, too
You, my Love, never have

Second Chances

If I could do it over
I'd still choose you
Knowing all your faults
I'd still choose you
Having faced our challenges
I'd still choose you
Given freedom and travel
I would still, always choose you

Big Love

It has never been about
What you do for me
It has always been about
How you treat me
As a friend and a partner
As a companion and a lover
As a spouse
You have never once failed
To treat me with respect
Honor
Kindness
I only hope I've done the same

Let Me Count The Ways

If I spend every day
Telling you of my love
We will still never cover it all
For every day
It grows Exponentially

What Are The Odds

15

We are not the same people
Nor are we opposites
More like two planets
Orbiting side by side
In outrageous unlikeliness
We share stars, and space
That has always been enough

Miss You

Cuddles in the dark
Embracing in the day
Forehead kisses lingering
Nothing left to say
Silent hours comforting
Talks from car to home
Wishy washy choice making
Walking just to roam
Plans well laid and executed
Last minute trips to the store
Day after day in your company
The minute you're gone, I want more

You Don't Know Until You Know

Love is hard to write
Words never seem quite right
Nothing spoken conveys the heart
It only shows real love in part
The rest, can only be felt

Transformer

I complain so things will change
I whine and I moan
I nag and I hassle
I push for how I think things should be
You never do
You accept
I wish I could explain to you
How much I look up to you
Your ability to take it all
Accept it
And give back love

Longing Never Goes Away

How can one person
Inspire so much
It seems unnatural
For just your touch
To so consume
My heart and mind

Yet here I sit
I think you'll still find
With a whole world to contemplate
My eyes remain blind
To anyone but you my Love
As I sit here, and I pine

Peacocks

It's all consuming
This feeling
In the mirror, grooming
For thine eyes alone

Oh, The Places We've Been

To be loved by you
Has been without a doubt
Some of the best moments
So don't you dare pout
Each moment spent beside
Your perfect body and intellect
Has been the highlight
Of a life devoid of regret
Wherever I am and wherever you are
It will never ever be too far
For me to forget the time we've spent
All the many universes we went
Scattered across all of time and space
Are pieces of me and you
Finding and adventuring
An endless party of two
We created an entire multiverse
Where versions of us exist
You and I are never alone
The love we share will always persist

www.ingramcontent.com/pod-product-compliance
Lightning Source LLC
Chambersburg PA
CBHW070730160726
48003CB00006BA/2424